IVANA INTERNATIONAL

Guide to Thriving

educational programme devised by Ivana Straska

 England

Guide To Thriving

All rights reserved. No parts of this book may be reproduced, scanned or distributed in any printed or electronic form without the written permission of the author. Please do not participate in or encourage piracy of copyrighted material in violation of author's rights. Purchase only authorized edition.

Neither the author nor the publisher is engaged in rendering professional advice or service to the individual reader. Information in this book is intended to educate and is not to substitute consulting with medical professionals. All matters regarding your health require medical supervision. Neither the author nor the publisher shall be liable or responsible for any loss or damage allegedly arising from any information or suggestion in this book.

First edition

ISBN 978-1-9998266-7-3

Cover design by Christopher Gill

Copyright © 2018 by Ivana Straska

Developed by IVANA INTERNATIONAL, England

IVANA INTERNATIONAL

guide to thriving

effective groundwork, emerging from individual uniqueness, eminently practical, simple

These pages introduce a programme intended to help in maintaining a high level of mental wellness at time when many people suffer through stress, or simply the pressure of modern time.

Guide To Thriving

It should be emphasised that this programme does not substitute counselling or treatment of mental health conditions. This educational programme is suitable for companies and private individuals to increase mental and emotional strength and flexibility. It is delivered in personal or online formats.

Guide To Thriving

"Study the heart and the mind of man, and begin with your own. Meditation and reflection must lay the foundation of that knowledge, but experience and practice must, and alone can, complete it."

- Lord Chesterfield, Letter to his son, June 6, 1751

Guide To Thriving

IVANA INTERNATIONAL

guide to thriving

Guide To Thriving

IVANA INTERNATIONAL

The following pages introduce the training programme by Ivana International. Flexible presentations, seminars, workshops and one-to-one sessions are delivered personally and/or distantly using online technologies.

Companies and individuals are welcomed to find additional information at www.ivanaint.com

Guide To Thriving

IVANA INTERNATIONAL

preface

Guide To Thriving

Having a positive work life is a natural desire for most adults, yet there are many struggles at work. When individuals wish to improve their experience, they do it through increased knowledge and skills. "Guide to Thriving" is an educational programme consisting of simple knowledge and techniques to strengthen mental performance. It targets the development of mental elasticity and resistance, which are the necessary skills for efficiently responding to difficulties, without undermining mental health.

This approach builds upon science and the facts that mental illnesses are more likely to occur as a response to circumstances, and largely to a predisposed population. With this simple programme, it is possible to develop understanding and skills in order to progress. By promoting mental wellness, the employer and employee mutually benefit. They create a thriving, healthy, more effective and inspiring place of work.

Adults typically fluctuate both mentally and emotionally. Being unaware of missing psychological strength and flexibility, and under pressure, people might experience mental conditions, which gradually worsen and require medical attention. This disadvantage is overcome through the "Guide to Thriving" programme.

Guide To Thriving

Introduction

Guide To Thriving

In recent years, the financial and human cost of mental illness in the productive generation has been sky-rocketing. There are more people at work with mental illnesses than ever before. According to independent U.K. government review* the overall annual costs of mental health to employers is between £33 billion and £42 billion. Almost all organisations share the human and financial burden resulting from mental illnesses. It is manifested through employees being less productive with poorer performance, and from fluctuations in workforce and staff turnover.

Common mental disorders are sometimes influenced by genes, but they are more likely to occur as a consequence or response to circumstances in life. Poor mental health often develops through an unrecognised psychological predisposition. Mental flexibility and strength are necessary skills for effective responses within the workplace.

Adults who are less psychologically resistant and inflexible might be unable to adequately cope with difficulties. They are often unaware, or they ignore or deny personal challenges. Without understanding, they may take incorrect actions and decisions thus building up problems. This disadvantage does not make people mentally ill but it makes them psychologically less efficient. Unaware of their limited life-skills, their mental health deteriorates making them prone to developing mental illness.

*Thriving at Work. The Stevenson / Farmer Review of Mental Health and Employers, October 2017, source:
https://assets.publishing.service.gov.uk/government/uploads/system/uploads/attachment_data/file/658145/thriving-at-work-stevenson-farmer-review.pdf

Guide To Thriving

Mental health fluctuates and a predisposition to mental illness often manifests under the pressure of work, stress, after loss, or when facing unexpected challenges. If conditions remain unimproved, over time, this tendency may intensify, and full-blown mental sickness requiring medical attention can result. With simple training and practise, individuals can overcome this disadvantage. They can fluctuate less between highs and lows, and take responsibility for their own mental well-being.

Organisations and employers can help in the promotion of mental well-being by the approach which:

~ targets current mental performance within the workforce, their resilience and resistance.
~ encourages employees' awareness of mental strength and susceptibility to mental deterioration.
~ provides strategies to decrease the risk of developing mental illnesses.
~ focuses on psychological strengthening and improvement.
~ assists employees to develop skills and knowledge to stabilise mental health.
~ provides the tools to maintain mental well-being and prioritise psychological resistance and flexibility.

Employers benefit by preventative training, helping both themselves and their workers to maintain performance and prevent illness. By prioritising and promoting mental wellness, employers help workers to develop awareness, knowledge and new skills.

Companies move towards a society with a common understanding of personal mental functioning. Employees increase responsibility for their mental well-being, and companies reduce the human and financial cost of mental illness.

A psychologically strong and resilient work force will positively add to company health. When feeling supported, a worker will improve their performance and productivity.

By promoting mental wellness, the employer will develop a healthier, happier, more efficient workforce more committed to their workplace. The employer and employee mutually benefit through providing a thriving, healthy, more effective and inspiring place of work.

Guide To Thriving

IVANA INTERNATIONAL

why do we need this training?

Guide To Thriving

The programme "Guide to Thriving" offers encouraging help to a spectrum of problems. With the application of evidence-based strategies, it assists organizations to helping workers by training them and strengthening their mental functioning. It aims to develop confident workers capable of utilise their psychological potential. It aids companies minimise the risks of developing of mental illnesses at workplace.

This approach is supported by science and experience. People can increase their psychological functioning when they learn constructive ways of thinking, modify non-efficient coping skills, and activate functional behaviour. Generally, people desire to succeed and have positive experience. With some knowledge and effort, they can thrive at work.

Because majority of individuals lack basic knowledge, they join the workforce without having an understanding of how thinking, emotions and behaviour affect their mental well-being or sickness. The programme "Guide to Thriving" increases this knowledge and helps workers to develop new skills. Through training, they strengthen their mental and emotional health, and prevent its deterioration.

This programme helps organizations focused on the prevention of mental sickness to transfer attention from psychological intervention to the strengthening of their employees. Training guides towards recognizing weaknesses in mental functioning, and strategies to build resistance.

Employees can develop skills that will positively influence their work, relationships and tolerance of stress. Skills enhancing mental flexibility and strengths are critical in lowering the risk of mental illnesses.

The programme modifies strategies successfully used in psychology and education. By the application of specific techniques, people learn how to help themselves and what to do to prevent worsening their mental health.

All this improves personal psychological capabilities and people begin to increase their thriving at work. They build responsibility for personal mental health. They receive tools and learn to commit to mental wellness. In return, employees feeling supported by their employers, stay at work and improve their performance.

Section 1
modification of thinking patterns

Guide To Thriving

F. D. Roosevelt said that people are not prisoners of their fate but of their mind. Indeed, what happens in the minds of people has enormous impact on their work and life. The ways in which people think play a critical role in how they respond to life and difficulties. The improved ways of thinking enhance beneficial behaviour and healthy decisions. Non-constructive, destructive and dysfunctional ways of thinking halt beneficial behaviour. They undermine mental health.

They ways in which people think develop throughout their lives. Individuals have typical patterns of thinking. Without acknowledgment, non-constructive thoughts have incapacitating impact.

Many attributes related to work are impossible to change and some people are unable to distinguish them. When they focus on uncontrollable aspects, wrongly interpret and focus on difficulties by themselves, problems escalate.

If ways of thinking are improved, emphasis turns to changed focus, correct interpretation and problem solving. This positively affects adaptability, adjustment, stress resistance and coping skills. Overall, this importantly assists mental functioning and general health.

When people acknowledge their thinking patterns, they can improve them. With a little knowledge and practise, they can develop thinking patterns that positively influence them and those around. People become more able to handle unexpected events. They improve their communication and social skills, while becoming less reactive and creating quality relationships. They think more positively and feel more fulfilled. Better ways of thinking increase efficiency and positive attitude, which consequently reduces risks of illness.

People think between fifty to seventy thousand thoughts daily. They get use to their own thinking, and they tend to believe their thoughts. People with low mental flexibility think non-constructively and their thinking patterns contribute to dysfunctional behaviour. They inaccurately interpret experience, the world and actions of others. They habitually respond inefficiently: regardless of circumstances, they might be too reactive and defensive, focused on wrong aspects and take incorrect actions. Overall, these limitations complicate and negatively affect their mental health.

Developing new thinking patterns allows modification of behaviour. Healthy mental patterns are necessary for health. Through the programme "Guide to Thriving", individuals can correct their ways of thinking and learn techniques to modify dysfunctional patterns. The goal is to increase mental flexibility, which decreases risks of mental ill health.

Additional aspects targeted by this programme are alleged false mental alarms and psychological biases. They can go unnoticed until they incapacitate individuals. This often happens when people develop mental illnesses.

Conveyed through generations, people are naturally inclined to think negatively for self-protection. Sometimes this tendency develops into false alarms. This means they perceive neutral events as danger and inappropriately respond to them.

They experience mental urges to defend or fight, and sometimes they act upon them. This consequently triggers wrong actions contributing to problems. Psychological biases and false alarms can be corrected through training.

Once people modify their thinking, they respond to work and life more accurately. Altogether, this approach enhances mental flexibility and decreases the chances of mental illness.

Guide To Thriving

Section 2
Working with beliefs

Guide To Thriving

To improve mental resilience this programme pays attention to rigid thoughts, which have disabling effect on individual psychological functioning. These are called beliefs, inflexible thoughts that start as principles and grow into personal guidelines. They function as internal psychological law regulating thinking, decisions, choices and actions.

Beliefs develop through experiences and knowledge. People do not attend to beliefs but they comply with them. Along with beliefs, people create solid emotional connections, affection and aversion. These emotional aspects make people more rigid, and with incorrect beliefs, they become psychologically impairing. They have destructive impact on mental performance, and often evoke people think and behave defensively.

People commonly do not acknowledge their beliefs, and they may blend beliefs with truth or reality. Problematic beliefs are big obstacles to self-improvement and contribute to mental instability. Surprisingly, people do not hold beliefs because they are correct. Rather, the beliefs somehow work in the individual's mental world. False beliefs can distort mental performance. Due to wrong beliefs, people misinterpret experience and take wrong actions.

Although beliefs can be strong, people can change and correct them. Through this programme, they learn how beliefs work in psychological functioning. Individuals practise techniques to restructure incorrect beliefs, and balance their belief system.

Guide To Thriving

section 3
activation of behavioural Change

Guide To Thriving

The third aspect significantly influencing mental performance is behaviour. Circumstances play roles and affect people, however more critical is how people react in response. Beneficial behaviour, actions people take positively contribute to events, is not natural to many individuals.

Constructive behaviour, something people can develop, moderates impacts of negative events. By taking correct actions, people also positively affect their mental performance. With understanding the consequences of behaviour, people grow an awareness of their behavioural patterns and capability to change.

Individuals predisposed to the occurrence of mental illnesses require training and strategies to optimise their reactions. This programme uses techniques of behavioural activation and targets functional and beneficial behaviour.

Behavioural activation helps to develop particular skills necessary for mental and emotional strengthening. With this programme, people learn to better deal with difficulties, and perform behaviour with positive influence. They learn to distinguish, control and efficiently react.

Behavioural activation emphasises self-improvement and weighing consequences. People practise to focus on controllable aspects and how to respond to limits. They exercise techniques to increase stress tolerance and acceptance. This consequently enhances their mental functioning and work performance.

Through training, individuals learn to engage effective behavioural reactions. They learn to consciously resist, regulate, chose and perform behaviour moving towards resolution or improvement. To establish new behavioural habits individuals practise to enforce behavioural change.

Dr. Viktor Frankl, a neurologist who studied human behaviour and survived the Holocaust, identified mental freedom of choice and having meanings as two critical phenomena people need for survival and thriving. Once people do not have freedom of choice and meaning, they lose hope and they give up. Mental freedom of choice comes from the correct thinking patterns and focus.

Individuals must take intentional effective actions to be mentally strong. Once they acknowledge meanings, even in difficult conditions, they can take correct actions helping them to succeed. This programme provides the strategy enforcing change. This highly assists to people who have higher risks of development of mental illness.

To accomplish behavioural change, the programme targets mental strengthening through personal goals. In this respect, SMART goals become a strategy towards improvement. SMART goals target changing behaviour and establishing new habits. Goals give meanings and guidance. They are checkpoints helping to maintain correct directions.

Through the development of particular skills, people exercise beneficial behaviours, which reduce fluctuation of mental states.

Performing actions that enforce change improves one's coping mechanism. People establish new behavioural patterns and this consequently improves their work. With new behaviour, people adapt faster and become mentally resistant. They decrease risks of development of ill mental health.

Guide To Thriving

section 4
emotional management

Guide To Thriving

To decrease the risks of mental ill health, people have to cope with their feelings and emotions effectively.

Feelings and emotions are natural and vital human experiences. However, the misunderstanding of feelings may impose unhealthy emotional processing. In fact, majority of adults fail to recognize their feelings as normal and functional responses.

People predisposed to develop mental illnesses often lack the skills to process emotions and feelings without letting them grow into complicated mental states. To decrease the risk of ill mental health, they must learn strategies of emotional processing through emotional management.

Emotions and feelings tend to grow complex and difficult to handle when they remain unrecognized. Emotional management teaches people to acknowledge, understand and regulate emotions and feelings. They learn to respond to emotions as temporary states, and process them effectively.

This means, they build knowledge and skills to adjust their emotional state without wearing down. Emotional management provides strategies helping individuals to strengthen and develop emotional flexibility and resistance.

Science supports emotional management because emotions are not built into the brain at birth (as many people think). Humans are born with abilities to feel, however, the type of emotions and when people experience them, are influenced by many factors.

The brain activates certain feelings and emotions in response to appraisal. In repetition, the brain creates pathways and overtime, specific emotions and feelings can become typical to an individual. Emotions do not seemingly happen to people, rather they develop as predictions of the brain.

Nevertheless, people can learn to regulate and control their feelings. Through emotional management, they learn about emotions as manageable, controllable states. They acknowledge feelings when they occur and use the techniques to regulate them.

Emotional management decreases risks that basic emotions stay unnoticed and grow into more difficult to manage states.

Unpleasant feelings are often associated with negative events and emotions might be unwanted reminders. It seems logical to avoid them, but avoidance used as strategy fails. Negative feelings return, and mostly in more severe and intense forms.

Unknowingly, people trap themselves. In attempts to banish negative feelings, they develop stressful vigilance causing inaccurate reactions in neutral events. Emotional management helps fix these unhelpful habits.

A suspect population tends to use avoidance and vigilance as coping mechanism, which consequently worsens their mental functioning. When people do not recognize negative feelings as normal states, they are prone to over-react and not to deal with causes. At times people do not discriminate emotions from thinking, and this distorts their reactions. All these increase probability of occurrence of ill mental health.

Emotional management teaches to acknowledge emotions and work with them as they are. This means, the participants learn to relate to their own feelings, which are different from feelings of the other people. They practise to recognize minds of others, which again differ from their own. The skills participants develop through emotional management significantly improve their emotional flexibility. They can advance and maintain personal psychological strength.

Guide To Thriving

Section 5
Confidence

Guide To Thriving

Individuals feel somehow about their abilities, skills, tasks, roles and functions, and to believe into personal capabilities is not natural to some people.

Mental and emotional fluctuation decreases confidence into personal resources. It undermines psychological functioning and negatively influences mental resistance. This programme helps to develop skills necessary for confidence.

The programme "Guide to Thriving" assists people to be better equipped and build some level of competence. Confidence grows from constructive beliefs. Through training, the participants of this programme can develop problem solving and decision-making skills. This positive change increases professional and personal performance, and consequently it enhances mental strength.

Confidence is not a personality trait, as people might think. It is a feeling generated by beliefs and skills. Confidence is an important component of psychological health, and it comes from a person's believing in their own abilities. Balanced thinking and beneficial behaviour heighten confidence.

Confidence is necessary to optimise one's mental functioning and perform well. Knowledge and skills are important, but lack of confidence undermines success. Wrong thinking patterns, ineffective behaviour and emotions can maintain low confidence.

People feel less confident about the unknown, about something new or potentially difficult. As this programme focuses on the development of functional skills, once people develop them, they change how they think and feel about themselves. They develop trust into their own capacities.

Confident individuals become valuable workforce members. They positively respond to challenges or mistakes, which they use as learning opportunities. Confidence spreads when confident people learn from other confident people. Confident individuals become role models for others and they let their confidence "rub off on them".

An essential part of building confidence is making accurate decisions and choices. With the correct techniques, people can learn how to balance decisions, and what to do to enforce beneficial choices. Accurate decisional and choice-making processes require stable thinking, commitment and ability to act upon a course of decisions. Building confidence is empowering strategy companies can use to strengthen their workforce.

This programme teaches how to engage thinking and behaviour that positively affect confidence. It reduces self-sabotaging non-constructive mental and behavioural habits. The programme also helps to modify expectations of how well or poorly circumstances work for or against an individual.

This programme elaborates other influential factors such as preparation, personal development, time management and skills necessary for mental stability. The participants learn how a positive mindset and optimism help to cope with challenges and maintain mental resistance. They learn how to heighten confidence and be confident not only in specific areas but also to believe into personal potential. This programme helps companies to create workplace where confident employees can thrive.

Guide To Thriving

section 6
relationships

Guide To Thriving

Unhealthy relationships are big challenges that negatively affect mental health. To create good relationships can be easier for some people, while others may struggle with this task.

Mentally and emotionally unstable individuals create rather stressful social interaction. They have difficulties to be flexible or tolerate limits. Dysfunctional thinking and behavioural patterns affect how people relate to each other. They may not understand how personal contribution worsens a relationship, or how they add to tension. All these reflect in their limits to create good relationships, including relationships at work.

Not all adults are aware of how they function socially. Psychologically vulnerable individuals may miss the ability to create good relationships at work because of their non-constructive thinking patterns, false beliefs, wrong expectations and standards, and much more. Mental and emotional instability always make relationships worse.

This programme aims good work relationships and the development of necessary skills to create them. Most of individuals are capable to minimize social deficiency when they develop new skills.

Good relationships require some social skills, effort, work, and importantly individuals who are capable to maintain quality relationships. Mental flexibility enhances self-control and improves social interaction. Individuals are prone to weigh consequences of their actions. They increase awareness and wiliness to offer positive contributions to relationships. They are more capable to adjust, tolerate, respect, or agree; all of which decrease stress and positively affect work relationships.

When people improve their psychological performance, they learn how to add to good relationships. They increase responsibility for relationships, and they become more capable to understand boundaries and limits.

Section 7
Communication
assertiveness

Guide To Thriving

Sending correct messages to other people, and correctly read the messages of others, is critical at a workplace. Wrong messages expressed verbally or with the use of body language can have profound consequences at a workplace. Verbal and non-verbal communication includes context, which also influences meaning and understanding of communication.

People predisposed to ill mental health have difficulties to effectively communicate. They cannot easily articulate their ideas and opinions. They find hard to react to disagreements, or express when they are not capable to meet requests. They often express themselves inaccurately and misinterpret actions of others.

Problematic thinking patterns limit abilities to talk about some topics such as feelings. Unjustified restrictions such as unrealistic fears, worries, guilt, shame or embarrassments negatively affect understanding and communication.

Assertive behaviour is ability to speak and act without breaking personal rights. This includes showing respect, balanced beliefs and beneficial actions. People, who tend to hold non-constructive thinking and behavioural patterns, may miss the aptitude to establish themselves without violating other people's or their own rights.

Assertiveness and effective communication are important skills at a workplace. They can be developed at any time and individuals suspected to mental illnesses should proceed with this training. They can restructure their thinking and behavioural patterns which impair communication and social skills.

Once people advance, they can contribute to work in effective ways. They become more understandable, consistent and transparent in relationships. The change helps them to improve work performance and relationships. Most importantly, it strengthens their mental health.

This programme allows employers to target communication skills as a strategy of decreasing risks of mental illnesses. Training of effective communication and assertiveness enhances mental strength and improves mental functioning of employees.

When people develop effective communications skills, they are more successful at work. They can contribute to quality relationships and improved work performance.

mindful Workplace

Guide To Thriving

"Carefully watch your thoughts, for they become your words.
Manage and watch your words, for they will become your actions.
Consider and judge your actions, for they have become your habits.
Acknowledge and watch your habits, for they shall become your values.
Understand and embrace your values, for they become your destiny."
~ Mahatma Gandhi

During the past years, mental health has gained an increased amount of attention, both from employers and employees. This attention has resulted in many valuable insights in what negatively contributes to mental health, and what causes psychological deterioration.

Mental health fluctuates between good and bad. The pressure of modern life, frequent changes, unexpected challenges and losses intensify the battle. There is no reason to wait until mental conditions conflict with life and work. There is another way to move forward, to fluctuate less between highs and lows, and this programme provides the way.

Guide To Thriving

IVANA INTERNATIONAL

about the founder

Guide To Thriving

The programme "Guide to Thriving" has been developed by Ivana Straska (Szakal), M.A., the founder of Ivana International, counsellor, educator and author of self-help books.

As her response to the steep rise of mental illnesses, Straska developed the programme "Guide to Thriving" to direct attention towards improvement of mental health.

In one way or another, almost every organisation shares the costs of the rapid increase in mental illnesses. Straska believes that with effective focus on prevention of mental illnesses both the employer and employee can profoundly benefit. Importantly, she developed this programme to help the productive generation increase their psychological resistance and flexibility.

Straska wrote three self-help books "The Strongest You", "Mindfulness, Breathe In – Breathe Out", "Confident Me" to increase awareness of the ways of thinking and behaviour, which critically influence psychological performance. The books introduce and teach easy to apply techniques, understanding the mind and feelings, and taking new actions. These are achievable goals for anyone who wants to create a healthier and happier experience.

Now residing in Yorkshire, England, Ivana Straska (Szakal), M. A., a successful educator and mental health professional, was formerly located in the Greater Toronto Area, Ontario, Canada. She grew up, obtained her degrees and first work experience in Bratislava, Slovakia (the former Czechoslovakia) where she was born.

She launched her private practice in Toronto in 2008 when she became a member of The Association of Registered Psychotherapists & Mental Health Professionals (O.A.C.C.P.P.), Dalton Associates, Psychological & Counselling Services in Ontario. Shortly after, she joined GTA Psychological Services and extended her practice from Greater Toronto Area throughout Halton and Waterloo Regions, Ontario. With the development of online services, she has been working with clients, both in Canada and around the world.

Her expressed purpose has always been to help people experience the greatest possible fulfilment in their lives, and her work has grown into her passion. Her qualifications are augmented by extensive knowledge in the fields of education, behavioural science, cognitive and behavioural therapy, mindfulness and mental imagery, all of which enforce her professional credibility.

She brings inspiration and her unique style to help others. Her work and practise consist of both altruistic and commercial projects targeting improvement of mental and emotional health.

Contact İnformation

Guide To Thriving

IVANA INTERNATIONAL

Contacts

Telephone: +44-8452-872-664

Website: www.ivanaint.com

E-mail: info@ivanaint.com

Location: Yorkshire, England

Books & audio sales

www.TheStrongestYou.net/buy-now

More about associated projects

www.TheStrongestYou.net

www.Feel-Good.xyz

www.MCWorld.me.uk

www.ingramcontent.com/pod-product-compliance
Lightning Source LLC
Chambersburg PA
CBHW071727020426
42333CB00017B/2419